Living in
MAKKAH
مكة المكرمة

Shadiya Sugich

Macdonald

Managing editor: Belinda Hollyer
Series and book editor: Polly Dunnett
Series designer: Sally Boothroyd
Book designer: Danuta Trebus
Picture researcher: Suzanne Williams
Production controller: Marguerite Fenn

Consultants: Mai Yamani
Aisha Gouverneur

Ismail Bin Haji Abdul Halim
B.A., M.A. (Lecturer: The
National University of Malaysia
and The Muslim College,
London)

A MACDONALD BOOK
© Macdonald & Company 1987
First published in Great Britain in 1987
by Macdonald & Company (Publishers) Ltd
London and Sydney
A BPCC plc company
All rights reserved
Made and printed by
Henri Proost, Belgium

Macdonald & Company (Publishers) Ltd
Greater London House
Hampstead Road
London NW1 7QX

We would like to give special thanks to the
Islamic Texts Society for their help and
advice during the preparation of this book.

We would also like to thank Gai Eaton of the
Islamic Cultural Centre at the London
Mosque for his comments on the manuscript,
and Dr G. R. Hawting of London University's
School of Oriental and African Studies for his
help with the history.

BRITISH LIBRARY CATALOGUING IN PUBLICATION DATA

Sugich, Haroon
    Living in Makkah—(City Life)
    1. Makkah (Saudi Arabia)—Social life
    and customs—Juvenile literature
    I. Title II. Series
    953'.8 DS248.M4

ISBN 0-356-10327-7

Artist
Chris Forsey 42–43

Photographic sources
Key to position of pictures:
(T) top, (C) centre, (R) right
(L) left, (B) bottom

Camerapix: 17T, 18BL, 20–21, 23TR, 24, 24–25,
    26–27B, 27T, 27CR, endpiece.
Faarid Gouverneur; 9BR, 12–13B, 18–19T & B, 40
I.P.A. Picture Library: 8BL, 9TR, 13R, 27B
I.P.A. Picture Library/Royal Geographical Society:
    15B
Islamic Texts Society: Opposite title page, 12T
Islamic Texts Society/Chester Beatty Collection:
    10, 11TR & B, 13T, 14, 15T
Khalid Khidr: endpapers, contents page, 17C&B,
    18C, 20L, 21R, 22L, 23TL, & CR, 25B, 26, 26–
    27T, 34L&R, 35, 36–37, 38T&B, 39
NAAS: cover, title page, 8–9T, 16, 19TR&C, 22R,
    23BL&R, 27CL, 32B, 33T, 41B
Peter Sanders: 25T, 32T
Frank Spooner Pictures: 41T
Haroon Sugich: 10–11T, 28, 28–29, 29B, 30BL,
    33CL, 37T
Shadiya Sugich: 29T, 30BR, 33CR
Helen Sugich: 30T, 31.

Cover picture: An aerial view of Makkah at the time of the Hajj (pilgrimage). The Holy Mosque and surrounding streets are flooded with pilgrims.

Endpapers: Pilgrims circling the Ka'bah create a whirlpool effect in this night-time photo.

Title page: A shopkeeper reads his Qur'an. His shop is closed for prayer-time.

Opposite title page: 'In the Name of God, the Merciful, the Compassionate.' This phrase, written here in Arabic calligraphy (decorative script), is used by Muslims before doing anything of any importance at all.

Contents page: A shopkeeper in traditional Saudi dress takes the air on the pavement outside his shop.

Page 44: The edge of the *haram*, or sacred, territory around Makkah. The notice reads 'Here ends *haram*' in Arabic and English.

Contents

The Holy City   8

Origins   10

Muhammad and Islam   12

Empires and kingdom   14

The Ka'bah and the Holy Mosque   16

The pilgrimage   18

Crossroads of the world   20

Markets and shopping   22

Pilgrim business   24

Patterns of the day   26

Family life   28

The Shafys   30

Growing up   32

Makkans relaxing   34

Seasons of the year   36

The Boom   38

Neighbouring places   40

Map of Makkah   42

Further information   44

Index   45

The Holy City

Makkah is unique. There is no place on Earth that is like this Arabian desert city, which is the very heart and centre of Islam. The religion of Islam has around one billion followers, or nearly one quarter of the world's population. Followers of Islam are called Muslims, and the fulfilment of the Muslim's life is a journey to Makkah, and the sacred places near by, to perform the rite of Hajj, or pilgrimage. This ritual takes place once every year in and around the city of Makkah.

Even those Muslims who are too poor to afford the journey cherish Makkah as Islam's most sacred city. Children from Muslim countries begin learning about Makkah in story and song from the time they are very small. And when they begin school they learn about events which took place in Makkah when Islam first appeared, for Makkah was the birthplace of Islam, and of its Prophet, Muhammad.

Above: The original village of Makkah lay in a valley surrounded by rocky hills. Today the town spreads far beyond the bounds of the valley, covering even the hills, and extending out into the parched and rugged desert.

Left: The tall buildings around the Holy Mosque in Makkah are hotels and other places for pilgrims to stay. Recently, the king of Saudi Arabia ordered that all the buildings in the centre of Makkah should be painted white, as was the tradition in the past.

The Ka'bah

At the very heart of the city is the Ka'bah, an almost cubic structure, empty inside, which Muslims believe was first built in ancient times, for the worship of God. Every Muslim turns towards the Ka'bah five times each day in prayer, and it is because of the Ka'bah that Makkah is held in such high esteem.

Desert city

Makkah lies in and around a stony hollow in the western deserts of Saudi Arabia. It is a harsh terrain of rocky hills and valleys, made harsher by the blazing heat of the desert sun.

The hilliness of Makkah is one of its most striking characteristics. Makkans get used to walking up and down steep winding streets and pathways, leading to hillside residential districts. Some of the oldest areas of the town can only be reached by a seemingly endless series of steps.

Above: Only Muslims can enter the city of Makkah and the surrounding sacred area. Non-Muslim traffic is diverted around the city and police may examine the identification of travellers wishing to enter Makkah.

Below: There is always, at all times of the year, a huge crowd of worshippers around the Ka'bah, in the courtyard of the Holy Mosque in Makkah. For Muslims, the sanctuary of the Ka'bah is a place of peace and spiritual inspiration.

For Muslims only

For non-Muslims, perhaps the most puzzling and fascinating feature of Makkah is that they are not allowed to enter the city or even the surrounding territory. The whole area around Makkah is called *haram*, a word which means both forbidden and sacred. Only Muslims can visit or live in Makkah.

Why is this so? For Muslims, Islam is a complete way of life, encompassing even the most ordinary daily activities. The cities of Makkah and Madinah (its sister city to the north) provide a refuge for Muslims who want to experience Islam in its most complete form, without the interference and distraction of other beliefs, religious practices or lifestyles. It is as if Makkah and the whole area around were a shrine. Here Muslims from all over the world can come to practise the life patterns of Islam without any compromise.

Origins

Muslims believe that the valley of Makkah was chosen by God as a holy place at the beginning of time, and that the first settlement at Makkah was established when the Prophet Abraham was commanded by God to send his wife, Hagar, and their son, Ishmael, into the desert. This was an act of faith, by which Abraham entrusted his wife and son to God's care. By the time mother and child had exhausted their supply of water they had reached the spot that was later to become Makkah. Hagar searched for water to quench her child's thirst, running between two low hills which became known as Safa and Marwah. All the time she prayed to God for help and, in answer to her prayers, a spring of water burst forth miraculously from the dry earth beside the infant child. The spring became known as the well of Zamzam.

According to Muslim tradition, the presence of water attracted some people passing near by on their travels from Yemen. The people made a contract with Hagar for the use of the well, and thus a settlement was established. This was the origin of the first village of Makkah.

Muslims believe that Abraham later visited Makkah, and taught the people to worship one God rather than many different idols. At God's command he built the Ka'bah (with the help of Ishmael), and established the rites of pilgrimage.

Makkah was soon revered throughout Arabia as a holy place, and the pilgrimage became an annual institution.

The 'Age of Ignorance'

However, after the death of Ishmael, the people of Makkah gradually forgot the teachings of Abraham and they reverted to worshipping idols made of clay and stone. The annual pilgrimage continued, but it was corrupted by idol worship and accompanied by a trade fair. This long period, which lasted until Muhammad was called to be a Prophet, is known to Muslims as the *Jahiliyya*, the 'Age of Ignorance'.

Above: A bedouin man tends his camels near the super-highway approaching Makkah. For many centuries Makkah remained an outpost in this desert landscape. It was a stopping-place on the trading routes from Yemen to the south and Syria and Palestine to the north.

Right: The first settlers on the site of Makkah were nomadic bedouin people from Yemen. This picture from a 16th century Persian manuscript gives a fanciful image of bedouin life. The lady on the right is spinning, while sheep and goats graze near by. The details in the picture — such as the tent and the ladies' clothes — are all Persian in style.

A nomadic outpost

The early inhabitants of Makkah were Arabs from nomadic tribes, called 'bedouin'. Before settling in Makkah they had roamed the deserts of Arabia seeking pastures for their herds of camels and other animals, and they lived in tents that could easily be moved on. Bedouin tribes of this sort are led by a *sheikh*, who can only lead so long as he has the support of the people. There is no written law, but all members of the tribe have a duty to protect one another and to protect the honour of the tribe.

For centuries, the society of Makkah was very similar to that of these tribes, and the town – or village – remained little more than a cluster of tents around the Ka'bah. The Makkans, however, were a settled people, and did not continue the migrations of the Arab tribes of the desert.

The prosperity of Makkah

From the very beginning Makkah prospered. As well as the wealth it acquired from being a great centre of pilgrimage, it became important as a trading centre. The Makkans developed into skilled merchants trading in perfumes, incense, spices, seeds, glue, silks, oils, African slaves and ivory.

To protect themselves as they crossed the desert these merchants travelled in large groups, called caravans, with camels to carry their goods. Two caravans were organized out of Makkah: one in winter to the north and one in summer to the south. These caravans grew to enormous size and wealth, sometimes employing as many as 2 500 camels.

Above: This 16th century Turkish miniature shows the Ka'bah in pre-Islamic times, draped with a chevron, or zig-zag, patterned covering. The tradition of covering the Ka'bah began long before the coming of Islam. It is said that the first covering was made about 200 years before the time of the Prophet. Inspired by a dream, a Yemani king draped the sacred House with dried leaves, sewn together.

Eventually Makkah became a major market centre for all of Arabia.

Nearly two centuries before Muhammad was born, one ruler of Makkah ordered his people to build houses for themselves out of stone to replace their tents. As their wealth increased these homes became larger and grander, and the Makkans adopted many customs and practices from other lands.

But for all their wealth and culture, Makkans still worshipped idols. Immorality, and even cruelty, were common and this was to continue until the coming of the Prophet Muhammad.

Above: For centuries before the coming of Islam the people of Makkah worshipped idols. At the time when the Prophet Muhammad was born, hundreds of idols could be found at the Ka'bah. This picture from a 16th century Turkish manuscript shows broken idols at the base of the Ka'bah. They have been finally destroyed by the Prophet.

Muhammad and Islam

Muhammad was born in Makkah in 570 AD. He was orphaned as a young child and brought up first by his grandfather and later by his uncle. As a young man he was well known for his unusual truthfulness and wisdom, and he was one of the few people in Makkah who did not believe in idol worship, but tried instead to follow the original teachings of Abraham.

When he was in his 20s, Muhammad was hired by a wealthy widow, Khadija, to lead her caravans. Khadija admired this extraordinary young man and eventually they were married. They settled into a peaceful and prosperous family life.

Revelation and Prophethood

Muhammad was concerned about the idol worship, corruption and cruelty that he saw around him in Makkah, and he began to withdraw to the mountains for long periods of meditation and fasting.

When he was forty years old, he withdrew into a cave high on a nearby mountain, where he had a vision of the Archangel Gabriel, commanding him to: "Recite! In the name of your Lord . . ." From that moment Muhammad became a Prophet, or Messenger of God. He received revelations from God through Gabriel, and these revelations formed the Holy Qur'an, the sacred book of the religion called Islam.

Islam

Islam is a word meaning both submission and peace. According to its teachings, human beings can attain both inward and outward peace by submitting to the commands of God, or *Allah* (an Arabic word meaning *the* God). And, according to Islam, this peace and obedience leads to salvation and entry into Heaven. Muhammad was ordered to call all people to Islam.

It involves observing five 'pillars of faith'. These are: the firm belief in one God and in the Prophethood of Muhammad; regular ritual prayer, five times a day; giving alms to the poor and needy; fasting during the holy month of Ramadan; and the performance of the annual pilgrimage, or Hajj, once in every Muslim's life if at all possible.

Right: Whenever they mention the name of the Prophet, Muslims say, "May the peace and blessing of God be upon him." The phrase is written here in decorative Arabic script, under the words 'Muhammad the Messenger of God.'

Below: Jabal Nur, or 'Mountain of Light', just outside Makkah, where the Prophet Muhammad received the first revelations of the Qur'an.

Left: To begin with, the revelations of the Qur'an were memorized by the first Muslims, and recorded on skins, pieces of bone and on smooth stones, in an unsystematic way. Later, after the Prophet died, the revelations were compiled into a complete book – the Qur'an.

This page from a 10th century North African Qur'an is written in an early form of Arabic known as *Kufic*.

Below: The Holy Qur'an was revealed in the Arabic language. For Muslims, it is the word of God, pure and unchanged. All Muslims therefore learn to read the Qur'an in Arabic and use Arabic in their ritual prayers, no matter what their native language may be.

Here a pilgrim recites from the Qur'an in Arabic.

Resistance and persecution

These teachings were fiercely opposed by the ruling tribe of Makkah, who were the guardians of the idols in the Ka'bah. They were alarmed by Muhammad's growing number of followers, and they reacted by cruelly persecuting the weakest of them, forcing many to emigrate to Ethiopia where a Christian king gave them refuge.

After about ten years of hardship, Muhammad was invited to settle in a town called Yathrib, a few hundred kilometres to the north of Makkah. He accepted, and his departure is known as the *Hijra*, or migration. Yathrib was renamed Al Madinah (which simply means 'the city') and became the first capital of Islam.

The conquest of Makkah

In Madinah, Muhammad won new supporters for Islam and he was joined there by many of his followers from Makkah. The Makkans began to feel even more threatened by the growing number of Muslims, and several battles took place between the Muslims, now based in Madinah, and the Makkans. However, after some years, Muhammad and his followers were strong enough to lead an army into Makkah, and the Makkans, who by now had lost the will to resist, surrendered with hardly any fighting. Muhammad showed mercy towards the people of Makkah, who now accepted the teachings of Islam.

The peaceful conquest of Makkah was a turning point in the history of Islam. Many tribes who had been attracted to the religion had been hanging back, waiting to see whether Muhammad's own people in Makkah would finally accept his teachings. When they did, tribe after tribe throughout Arabia sent deputations to Madinah to declare their allegiance to Islam and its Prophet.

By the time the Prophet Muhammad died, all of Arabia had embraced Islam and word of the religion was beginning to spread still further.

Empires and kingdom

For thirty years after the Prophet Muhammad died (in 632 AD), Islam was ruled in succession by the four men who were closest to him: Abu Bakr, Omar, Uthman and Ali. They were called the Four Rightly Guided Khalifs, because they ruled with justice and in strict accordance with Islamic law.

During this time, and in the hundred years that followed, the influence and power of Islam grew rapidly until it had spread all the way across North Africa, into Spain and eastward through Persia to the borders of India and China.

The meeting place of many races

The dramatic expansion of Islam transformed the city of Makkah. Despite its remote situation and harsh desert character, it quickly became a cosmopolitan city, where people from all over the Muslim world gathered together, united by a common religion. Makkah was never a political capital, but it was always the spiritual centre of Islam – its longed-for city.

Islamic Empires

As the frontiers of Islam stretched, the capital moved from Madinah to Damascus and then to Baghdad. By this time the Islamic Empire had begun to split up into separate territories, ruled by local princes and generals, and Makkah came under the control of various Muslim rulers.

Gradually, three great Islamic Empires were formed: the Ottoman, or Turkish, Empire; the Persian Empire; and the Mughal Empire of India. For a long period Makkah was part of the Ottoman Empire, ruled by the sultans of Istanbul.

Left: This picture of the Ka'bah and Makkah was painted in the 18th century. It shows clearly how the buildings of the city clustered around the walls of the Mosque. These walls, with their series of domes along the top, survive today, though they are now surrounded by the newer –and higher – buildings of the Holy Mosque.

A closely-watched city

Because of its special importance in the Muslim world, Makkah tended to be a place where political refugees gathered, and many plots were hatched there against whoever was ruling the Empire at the time. This meant that the governors who were placed in charge of the Holy City tended to rule with an iron hand, sometimes depriving the citizens of their wealth, property and power.

The Arabs resented foreign rule, and some became bandits, waylaying caravans as they travelled to and from Makkah.

Saudi Arabia

In the late 18th century, armies led by a chieftain called Muhammad Ibn Saud gained control over Central Arabia. By 1802, they had conquered Makkah and Madinah, and for a little more than a decade, much of Arabia was united under one Arab leader – until Egyptian armies took over the Holy Cities and other parts of the peninsula.

It was not until this century that most of Arabia was united once more, under the leadership of Abdul Aziz Ibn Saud, a direct descendent of Muhammad Ibn Saud. Abdul Aziz became king of the tribes of Central Arabia, and by 1925 he had conquered Western Arabia, including Makkah. In 1932 the West and Central Kingdoms were united into a newly formed kingdom of Saudi Arabia, named after the ruling family.

Oil

In the 1930s King Abdul Aziz sold mineral exploration rights to an American oil company. Few people expected that anything of value would be found beneath the Arabian sands, but in 1938, after several years of drilling, Saudi Arabia had its first oil-producing well.

World War II interrupted the Kingdom's exploitation of its oil resources, but by the early 1950s the money from oil allowed Saudi Arabia to begin to develop into a modern industrial nation.

For Makkah, this meant that the Holy Mosque surrounding the Ka'bah was expanded, and the area immediately around it improved. This was a time when the first modern buildings began to replace the old traditional houses, and the first hotels were built to accommodate pilgrims.

Below: Abdul Aziz Ibn Saud (front left) united Arabia under the banner of Islam. The Saudi Arabian flag carries the creed of Islam: 'There is no god but God and Muhammad is the Messenger of God'.

A fearless warrior and brilliant desert politician, Abdul Aziz was commonly known simply as 'Ibn Saud'.

The Ka'bah and the Holy Mosque

The Ka'bah stands at the very centre of Makkah, and the town has grown up around it. It is the heart of the sacred city and thus of the entire Muslim world. It is the Ka'bah that all Muslims, wherever they may be, turn to face when they say their daily prayers.

The Battle of the Elephant

Muslims believe that Makkah has always enjoyed the protection of God because of the existence of the Ka'bah and there is a story referred to in the Qur'an which illustrates this special holiness. The story is called 'The Battle of the Elephant'.

In the very year that the Prophet Muhammad was born, a general named Abraha vowed to destory the Ka'bah. He set out towards Makkah with an army, but the citizens of Makkah made no attempt to defend themselves. They were not strong enough to stop the invading troops, and they believed God would protect the Ka'bah.

Sure enough, when Abraha's army reached the outskirts of the city, the elephant at the head of his army sat down and refused to move further. Then a flock of birds appeared in the sky, each one carrying stones in its beak and talons, which it hurled down on the army below. Anyone struck by a stone was killed instantly. The rest fled. Makkah was safe and the miraculous rout of Abraha's army is seen as proof of the Ka'bah's holiness.

The Ka'bah

The Ka'bah itself is a cube-shaped stone house built of stone and mortar. It is 15.25 metres high and empty inside. Built into the walls at the eastern corner is a Black Stone, said to have been blackened by the sins of human beings.

The Ka'bah is not meant to be entered; worshippers only circle round it. The massive raised doors are opened once a year for the ritual washing ceremony during the pilgrimage, or occasionally in honour of an important visitor.

The Ka'bah is covered with an enormous black silk cloth called the *Kiswat.* The cloth itself is woven into patterns of sacred Arabic script, and then more elaborate script is embroidered on the cloth in gold thread.

On the outside of the Ka'bah are two solid gold ornaments: the doors and the water spout. The doors are decorated with intricate tracery and verses from the Qur'an. They were made in the 1970s, and replaced the old doors that were made of 'aloes', a special sweet-smelling wood, and studded with silver.

A few metres from the Ka'bah, in the courtyard of the Holy Mosque, is a crystal case containing a stone. This is called the 'Station of Abraham' and the stone is said to

Above: The Ka'bah rises majestically above the worshippers around it. This is not the most crowded time of year, but still there are some pilgrims performing the *Umrah,* or smaller pilgrimage. The *Umrah* consists of circling the Ka'bah and running between the hills of Safa and Marwah.

be the boulder on which Abraham stood as he directed the building of the Ka'bah.

The Holy Mosque

The courtyard surrounding the Ka'bah is enclosed by the huge marble buildings of the Holy Mosque. This has grown over the centuries from a small area immediately around the House, to the enormous multi-storey complex that exists today. Nearly 500 000 worshippers can pray here at one time, and the Mosque is continually being added to and improved, even now.

The Holy Mosque is a focal point of life in the city and Makkans regard it as a meeting place as well as a sanctuary for prayer and meditation. Between sunset and night prayers, Makkans often meet at the Holy Mosque. They chat together, recite from the Qur'an, or simply watch the throngs of worshippers from every nation circling the Ka'bah. It is a fascinating and peaceful place to relax during the evening hours.

Left: The black silk *Kiswat* is handmade and replaced every year at huge cost. The cloth is handwoven, and then Arabic calligraphy (script) is embroidered on the cloth in gold thread – as in this picture. Each year the old *Kiswat* is cut up into pieces and sent to various Muslim organisations all over the world. Muslims like to have fragments of the *Kiswat* to frame and hang on the walls of their homes.

Left and above: Among the beautiful marble pillars of the Holy Mosque, hundreds of people relax and talk together, or simply sit quietly and read the Qu'ran. There are no separate areas for men and women, but according to Makkan custom they usually sit apart. The woman above is probably a pilgrim who has come with her family to perform the *Umrah*, or little pilgrimage.

The pilgrimage

Makkah would not be what it is without the pilgrimage, which is known in Arabic as *Al-Hajj.* According to the tradition of Islam, the Hajj was established by the Prophet Abraham, to whom it was revealed by God. It is the duty of all Muslims to perform the Hajj once in a lifetime, if they are able.

The rituals of the Hajj

The Hajj consists of a series of rituals which are based either upon the events that took place in the life of Abraham, or upon instructions from the Prophet. It must be performed in and around Makkah, on specified days during the Islamic month of Dhul Hijjah.

A male pilgrim must wear two seamless pieces of cloth, usually white, known as the *ihram.* (There is no similar rule for women, but they must not veil their faces.) From the moment that pilgrims begin their rituals, they must not cut their nails, remove any bodily hairs or kill anything, even an insect. They remain in this state until they complete the obligatory part of their rituals, and the effect of this is that everyone suddenly becomes outwardly the same – the rich, the poor, the young and the old. All are subject to the same rules and restrictions, and all are equal in the sight of God.

The main rituals of the Hajj include the *tawaf,* circling the Ka'bah seven times; the *sa'i,* running seven times between the two hills of Safa and Marwah to commemorate Hagar's search for water; standing on the plain of Arafat, near Makkah, in prayer and supplication; stopping at night on the plain of Muzdalifah on the way back from Arafat; and stoning three symbolic stone pillars in the valley of Mina, just outside Makkah.

A sea of worshippers

At the time of the Hajj, Makkah becomes a sea of worshippers, moving from place to place according to the stage the pilgrimage has reached. Pilgrims from every race and region of the world live in huge tent cities. The streets are flooded with people, and every available space is taken up with makeshift living arrangements. Many people must be content to sleep 10 or 15 to a room and all must suffer some discomfort among the crush of worshipping crowds.

Above: The single most important act of Hajj is to stand before God on the plain of Arafat, a few miles outside Makkah.

This picture focusses on the 'Mount of Mercy', a small hill rising out of the plain, where the Prophet Muhammad preached his last sermon.

Above: Pilgrims run between the hills of Safa and Marwah as they perform the *sa'i.* The course of the *sa'i* used to be open to the sky, but is now incorporated within the Holy Mosque.

Left: The *tawaf,* or circling the Ka'bah. At Hajj-time children and old people are often carried above the heads of the crowd to avoid being crushed.

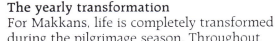

Above: Crowds of pilgrims on their way to Arafat. Many are carrying umbrellas – to protect them from the sun, not the rain!

The yearly transformation

For Makkans, life is completely transformed during the pilgrimage season. Throughout the month before the Hajj, city water is diverted from certain districts to fill the reservoirs of Arafat and Mina. Traffic gets heavier as busload after busload of pilgrims roll into town until, in the days immediately before the Hajj begins, the roads leading to Makkah become a steady stream of vehicles of every type.

The area around the Holy Mosque is cordoned off and no unauthorized cars are allowed to drive inside the city centre. Makkans must either remain inside the town, or leave their cars in the large car parks on the outskirts, and take public transport back and forth.

Pilgrims can be seen everywhere, walking alone or in groups, sitting in cafés and restaurants, crowding into shops, filling up every resting place in Makkah.

During this period Makkah no longer belongs to its residents but to the pilgrims. It is the pilgrims' city during Hajj-time, and Makkans have to make way for them and help them out whenever they can. For those who have been brought up in Makkah this is not only natural, but a pleasure. The Hajj is, after all, the livelihood of most Makkans, and they are serving Muslims who are experiencing the high point of their religious lives.

Because of both the wealth and the spiritual benefits it brings them, the Hajj is the best time of year for Makkans in spite of all its discomforts and difficulties.

Above: Two pilgrims rest and read the Qu'ran in the valley of Mina. They have completed the first phase of the Hajj and so have discarded the *ihram* in favour of ordinary clothes.

Left: As they travel to the different sites of the Hajj, pilgrims stay in huge 'tent cities' as in this picture.

Crossroads of the world

Below: The Nigerian neighbourhood of Makkah centres around Mansour Street. It is a maze of backstreets and pathways, full of the flavour of Africa.

You see Nigerian women sitting on pavements outside almost any public building in Makkah, selling nuts, sweets and trinkets. The children call them *Hajjah*. And many a neighbourhood is lulled by the sound of the dreamy, sing-song voices of Nigerian women selling their wares.

These Nigerian men have taken time off from driving their lorry to pose for a photograph.

One of the most striking characteristics of Makkah is its extraordinary mixture of cultures. In Makkah, you can hear many languages spoken, see people dressed in many different ways and buy all kinds of different food from Indonesian to European.

As the religious centre of Islam, Makkah has always been a city where Muslims of different nationalities converge to fulfil their spiritual obligations.

Even it's geographical position is at the very centre of a strip of Muslim countries that stretches half way across the world from Morocco in North Africa to Indonesia in South-East Asia. In fact, you could describe Makkah as the crossroads of the world.

Settlers from afar

Over the centuries, many Muslims who visited Makkah decided to settle there to be near the Holy Ka'bah. These settlers formed the nucleus of ethnic communities that still exist today. Gradually as the ethnic communities grew they took on a life of their own and whole neighbourhoods developed, consisting mainly of people from one particular part of the Muslim world.

In these neighbourhood communities you can find some people who come from families that have been settled in Makkah for several generations, some who have only recently arrived with residence permits to work in Makkah, and some who are pilgrims making only a brief visit.

To a very large extent, Makkans who can

trace their ancestors back to foreign lands still keep up ties with the countries they came from, and still keep to some of their original customs. Although every second or third generation Makkan speaks Arabic as a first language, many still speak the language of their forebears as well. Traditionally, settlers and their descendants have married within their own communities. Some families even send their sons back to their home country to find a wife.

These traditions are changing but the ethnic communities in Makkah are still very distinctive, and Makkans are still conscious of the differences in background that exist among them.

Right: Many Indonesian Makkans live in the Shamiyya district, near the Holy Mosque. Behind these Indonesian children you can see the remains of an old Makkan house which has been torn down to be replaced by modern buildings.

Below: Egyptians, Pakistanis, Senegalese, Yemanis, East Africans, Saudis, Syrians, Nigerians and Turks, all together in a street near the Holy Mosque.

Ethnic communities

Some of the oldest Makkan families bear Indian names, and many of the social customs that are associated with Makkan tradition actually derive from India. Makkans with Indian ancestry no longer live in a specific neighbourhood, but are spread through the centre of the town.

There are three other large ethnic communities in Makkah: Central Asian, Indonesian and African. Central Asians are known to Makkans as the 'Bukharis' because many emigrated from the Central Asian city of Bokhara. But the Bukharis consist of a wide variety of people, mostly from what is now southern Russia.

The Indonesian community are known among Makkans as the 'Jawa', after the island of Java from where many of them come. The African community are called the 'Takarna', named after Takroor, which was the first Muslim kingdom in West Africa. The Takarna in Makkah come almost exclusively from the various tribes of Nigeria.

Each of these sub-communities has its own neighbourhood with its own distinct flavour, like a little piece of another part of the world.

Markets and shopping

From earliest times Makkah has been a trading centre. In the pre-Islamic period, market fairs formed part of the pilgrimage celebrations, and this link between trade and religion has never ceased. Islam encourages trading and some of the most saintly Muslims in history were merchants. Even the Prophet Muhammad was a trader as a young man. Indeed the thriving market in a place as remote and barren as Makkah has been seen as a sign of God's special favour upon the city and its inhabitants.

Market districts

The original markets in Makkah grew up in the area immediately surrounding the Holy Mosque. Some pilgrims would bring goods to sell to pay the cost of their return journey and, in time, permanent markets for these goods developed around the Mosque.

In recent years many of these old market areas have been pulled down to make way for the expansion of the Holy Mosque and other new developments. Merchants have moved their businesses to new districts on the outskirts of town where wide boulevards are lined with shopping centres, boutiques and supermarkets.

In stark contrast to the new shopping districts are the traditional Arab markets, which are still very much alive. The ancient *Souq Al Lail* (Night Market) is one of these; there are others in the districts of Ajyad, Shubaikah and Misfalah.

Buying in bulk

Makkans are accustomed to buying their food in bulk, often for a whole week or even a month at a time, and they may share out some of what they buy among their extended families. It is not unusual for a family to buy their fruit by the box. The same is true with meat, poultry and eggs.

Above: One of Makkah's two large *halaqa*, or fruit and vegetable markets. Food shopping in Makkah is nearly all done by men.

Above: Shopping is a favourite pastime among Makkan women, though they tend to leave the more dreary food shopping to the men. These women are buying prayer beads and may go on to buy cloth at the shop on the right, or gold at the shop on the left. Gold is considered to be a very important part of wealth in Saudi Arabia, especially for women.

Left: Although Makkah now has a few western-style supermarkets, most people still buy their provisions from neighbourhood shops like the one pictured here. For fruit and vegetables, however, they may go to one of the large *halaqa*.

Left: These women shoppers have covered their faces with the traditional Makkan veil, made of a thin, gauze-like material.

Styles of veil vary from region to region and country to country.

Many Makkan families buy a live sheep every two weeks or so, which they slaughter for the fresh meat. They give some to relatives and the rest they freeze to use up over the next couple of weeks.

Similarly, although frozen chickens are plentiful in shops, most Makkans prefer fresh chicken which they can pick out live from neighbourhood chicken shops to be killed and plucked while they wait. Usually, not far away from the chicken shop you can find the eggman and it would not be unusual to see a customer walk away with three dozen eggs.

Below: In the traditional market districts of Makkah, shops and stalls line the crowded pavements, their goods spilling out at passers-by in a haphazard jumble of colours and shapes. Bargaining – as in this picture – is common at such stalls.

Above: The Prophet Muhammad loved perfume, and Muslims follow his example. There are perfumeries all around the Holy Mosque.

Below: Street-sellers are a common sight on the pavements around the Holy Mosque. Pilgrims sometimes earn their keep in this way.

Pilgrim business

Below: During the Hajj-period eating places overflow with customers. Pilgrims often have their meals in makeshift dining areas, and this side-street banquet is typical.

Money-changing is an even bigger pilgrim-related business. Money-changers vary from the old-fashioned stallkeeper, propped up in little more than a hole in the wall, changing thousands of dollars an hour with flying fingers, to large modern offices. You can see a money-changer's sign in this picture, above a crowd of pilgrims waiting to change money.

The pilgrimage is a major part of the economic life of Makkah. In the past, it was a vital source of income for whoever ruled this part of Arabia, and pilgrims had to pay heavy taxes. Now, because of the oil wealth, Hajj fees are low, but the merchants of Makkah are as dependent as ever upon pilgrims. Today pilgrim trade comprises over half the income of most Makkan businesses.

Pilgrims arriving in Makkah may bring much of what they need with them but there are always things that they will buy on the spot: the white towelling used as pilgrim garb, plastic sandals, camera film, money belts specially made for pilgrims, inexpensive prayer carpets, plastic and wooden rosaries, pocket-sized Holy Qur'ans for reciting, instruction manuals explaining how to perform the pilgrimage rituals, cooking utensils, bottled water, and, of course, food.

Also, luxury goods are not highly taxed in Makkah as they are in many other countries.

This means that during Hajj-time, there is a run on wrist-watches, tape-recorders, kitchen appliances and many other products sold without the addition of high import duties or sales taxes. And, of course, most pilgrims want to buy gifts for their families and friends back at home, and at least one souvenir of their stay in Holy Makkah.

Considering that nearly two million visitors descend upon the city every year, for at least one week, it is easy to understand how important the pilgrim business is to the merchants of Makkah.

Pilgrim guides

The other important Hajj-related business is that of the pilgrim guide, called in Arabic the *mutawif*, which means, literally, one who leads people on the *tawaf*, or circuits round the Ka'bah. Pilgrim guides are specialists in leading pilgrims through their rituals as well as housing and feeding them.

Below: Many Makkans earn a little extra money by selling soft drinks during the pilgrimage season. Here pilgrims reach for cans of mixed-fruit juice and bottles of spring water to quench their thirst in the heat of the day.

Left: Indonesians are especially known for making the embroidered *kuftias*, or prayer caps, worn by men in Saudi Arabia. Here a family of Indonesian pilgrims are selling robes, caps and prayer scarves from bundles they have brought with them all the way from their home country. The money will help pay for their own journey.

Below: A pilgrim in suit and tie buys a souvenir before going home. Many pilgrims wear the traditional Muslim white robes while they are in Makkah, returning to western-style clothes when they leave the Holy City.

The bookshop in the foreground of this picture will specialise in selling copies of the Qu'ran and other religious books.

Traditionally, the *mutawif* profession was hereditary, passing from father to son. Nowadays, however, there are larger organizations, usually consisting of several families of pilgrim guides, and responsible to government agencies which make sure they are serving their pilgrims well.

Newer occupations

The development of pilgrimage facilities over the last two decades means that there are now more varied work opportunities for Makkans. Many people are employed to provide things like medical care for pilgrims, or postal and telephone services, or transport. Other new occupations include traffic control as well as simply cleaning and maintaining the new public buildings and walkways.

Patterns of the day

The Makkan day begins before dawn. At this time there is a stillness in the city broken only by crowing cocks, the bark of an occasional stray dog and the quiet hum of a police car patrolling to see that its assigned neighbourhood is safe. One hour before the dawn prayer, the first call rings out from the powerful loud speakers of the Holy Mosque. Inside houses alarms buzz, and as the time for the dawn prayer approaches, men slip out of their homes and make their way to the neighbourhood mosque or, if they live near the centre, to the Holy Mosque. Especially around the Holy Mosque, the streets begin to fill with worshippers moving quietly together to pray in congregation.

Prayers and heat

The pattern of daily life in Makkah is determined by two main considerations: the Muslim prayers and the desert heat. In Islam there are five obligatory prayers said at particular times every day, according to the movement of the sun.

The *subh*, or dawn prayer, is said when the first thread of light appears on the horizon; the *dhuhr*, or noon prayer, begins when the sun passes the highest point of the sky; the *asr*, or afternoon prayer, occurs about half way between high noon and sunset; the *maghrib*, or sunset prayer is said immediately after the sun has dropped below the horizon; and the *isha*, or night prayer, is said when twilight has left the sky and the night has become dark.

Because it is a holy city, the observance of prayer is considered particularly important in Makkah, and all the normal activities of the city stop during prayer-time. Muslims do not have to pray inside a mosque, and you often see groups of people praying in formation on mats inside their shops and offices or out on the pavement, or anywhere that is convenient and clean.

In Makkah, prayer times tend to mark out the day and serve as reference points. When people make appointments they often refer to the prayer-times, rather than to a specific hour: "I'll meet you after *dhuhr*", or "Come to supper after *isha*." In the past there was even a 'Makkah time', which was adjusted to the times of prayer. Clocks were re-set every day to exactly 12.00 at sunset, which is the beginning of the Islamic day. This form of time-telling used to be common in Makkah, but has now virtually disappeared. Still, you can find a few mosques with clocks set to 'Makkah time'.

As in most hot countries, heat plays a major role in the way people arrange their days. Even though almost everyone now enjoys the luxury of air-conditioning, most Makkans still tend to get up early and stay up late, saving a large part of the middle of the day to rest inside their homes.

Right: Shops in Makkah must close by law during prayer-times. Many shopkeepers simply stretch a cloth across their open store as the man in this picture has done. He is reading the Qu'ran after completing his own prayers.

Above this shop you can see some traditional wood carving that used to be typical of buildings in Makkah.

Right: An early morning scene. The long shadows show the sun is still low in the sky, so this is the time for essential jobs such as tending animals.

Mornings in Makkah are generally a quieter time than the late afternoons and evenings. The rising sun quickly brings an oppressive heat, which makes any out-of-doors activity very unattractive.

Left: Stallholders at one of Makkah's large fruit and vegetable markets set out their goods ready for early morning shoppers.

Left: The heat drives most Makkans indoors during the middle of the day. This picture was taken at mid-day in winter. In summer the windows, curtains and shutters would probably be closed, so intense is the light and heat.

Indoor plants are popular in some Makkan homes, though it is hard to keep plants alive when the temperature indoors varies between the extreme natural heat and the cold of the artificial air-conditioning.

Above: A street scene in the late afternoon. Shops re-open at about 5 p.m. and Makkah comes alive as the sun sets and evening winds cool down the simmering desert heat. The boy in the foreground of this picture is carrying a bottle of water from the well of Zamzam.

Right: The evening is a time of bustling activity in Makkah. Many shops stay open until about 10.30 p.m. and Makkans save their going about to this time of day, if they possibly can.

Left: The sunset prayer, or *maghrib*, around the Ka'bah. The people are standing ready for the prayer to begin.

The time between the sunset prayer and the night prayer, or after the night prayer, are the most popular times to meet around the Ka'bah, and enjoy the calm evening air after the blazing heat of the day.

Family life

In Makkah, life revolves around an extended family of parents, grandparents, cousins, uncles and aunts. The importance of the family in Makkan life stems partly from Arab tradition, but it is also a fundamental part of Islam. Bringing up a family is considered to be a Muslim's most complete way of living.

Marriage
Marriage is of great importance to all Muslims and in Makkah all marriages are arranged in the traditional way; that is, between the women of the boy's and girl's families.

When a young man becomes ready for marriage his mother and sisters ask around among relatives and friends for a suitable girl from a good family. When they hear of one, the boy's mother visits the girl's mother and if the meeting goes well, the girl's father and brother begin to make enquiries about the young man. They ask friends and neighbours about him, perhaps speak to his employer, and they may even go to his local mosque to see if he attends prayers regularly.

If both families are satisfied, a meeting is arranged between the boy and girl themselves, and if they like each other, marriage is proposed through the boy's mother. If the girl accepts the proposal,

Right: A Makkan mother helps her son with his homework. It is evening, and they are sitting out on the *satooh*, or roof garden, of their house, where they can enjoy the cool breezes.

arrangements are made for the marriage ceremony, or *milka*. There may then be a gap of a few months before the wedding party, or *farah* (meaning happiness).

At the *farah*, men and women gather separately and for the men it is a relatively uneventful occasion. For the women, however, it is a very special night. The bride and groom usually arrive together, but after presenting gifts to the bride and her family and cutting the wedding cake with his wife, the groom departs. The women stay on and are entertained deep into the night, often till dawn, by women singers and musicians.

Men and women
In Makkah, the roles of men and women are clearly defined, not only by local custom but also by Islamic teaching and practice. In Islam, men and women are completely equal, but they have different roles and duties. A man's first duty is to work and earn a living. A woman's first duty is to care for her home and bring up her children. Women are not prohibited from working, and many Makkan women now work as teachers, some as doctors and a few even own businesses, but working mothers still place their family responsibilities first.

The distinction between men and women is clearly reflected in traditional Saudi dress. In public men wear a long white robe, or *thobe*, and cover their heads with a small white skull cap. Over this they wear an ironed, folded triangular piece of cloth – either the red and white checked *shumach* or the white *ghutra* – held in place by a black circular *egaal*.

Below: Food is very important in Makkah and a lot of care is taken over preparing it. Although men do the shopping for food, women are in charge of planning meals. In fact, women generally control the purse-strings of the household, and a husband is in the service of his wife so far as the running of the home is concerned.

Islamic law requires women to cover their hair and necks and the rest of their bodies in public. Makkan women wear the black, flowing, cape-like *abaya* and, as in the rest of Saudi Arabia, many of them also veil their faces. Indoors, women do not wear a veil but if a male guest visits, they cover their hair with a voluminous white *sharshif*, or scarf, which is also used for prayer at home.

Close-knit family

Traditionally, an extended Makkan family would live in one large house or in smaller houses built close to one another. Sometimes a single large family would make up a neighbourhood. Family members would meet together often, eat their meals together and cousins would grow up together.

Some families still pool their incomes to save enough to build a large house which allows them to live together. But it is now more common for young couples to live in rented apartments, and most of the newly built housing is western in design and divided into flats. Families have tended to separate, spreading out through the town, but they still try to keep in close touch with each other. Grown-up children usually visit their parents at least once a week, and families often gather together to chat, drink tea and have an informal meal.

The close-knit family also serves as a form of social security. It is common practice in Makkah for grown-up children to support their parents in old age, with brothers and sisters sharing the financial burden.

Above: The Shafy family, including cousins, enjoy a picnic inside the courtyard of their new house. You can see the street beyond the wrought-iron gate in the background. This kind of family gathering is an everyday event in Makkah and children grow up surrounded by cousins and other relatives.

Left: When visitors come to a Makkan house, men and women meet separately. Here Ramzy Shafy (right) is sitting with the husband of one of the teachers from his wife's school, while the two women sit together in the next room. Meetings like this are relaxed and chatty.

The Shafys

The Shafy parents, Ramzy and Aisha, come from old Makkan families and both grew up in neighbourhoods next to the Holy Mosque. Both can trace their ancestry back to foreign lands. Ramzy's background is Indonesian; Aisha's father's family came from Afghanistan well over a century ago, and her mother came from Egypt. Aisha comes from a family of pilgrim guides (*mutawifeen*) and Ramzy works on her behalf in the *mutawif* business during the pilgrimage season.

Ramzy and Aisha are both teachers; Ramzy is the headmaster of a boys' school outside Makkah and Aisha is headmistress of a girls' high school in an outlying village. Their daughter Nashwa is 12 years old and in secondary school. She has two brothers: Ali, aged 6, who has just begun attending his father's school, and new born baby Raja who stays behind with the family servant.

Education is considered very important in Saudi Arabia and, as senior teachers, the Shafys are well paid compared with teachers in many other countries. Like many middle-income families in Makkah they can afford to employ a servant, Maryam, whom they brought all the way from Indonesia to take care of their house and children.

The daily routine

The Shafy family get up before the break of day, say their prayers and prepare for school. School starts at 7.30 a.m. in summer and 8.00 a.m. in winter, finishing at noon prayer-time or just after. Lunch is the main meal of the day for Makkans and the Shafys eat a large cooked meal of meat and rice or some kind of pasta, with a variety of vegetable

Above: Lunch-time in the Shafy house. The curtains are drawn to shut out the mid-day sun and the family sit on the floor in traditional fashion, with a variety of dishes set out on a cloth. This is a typical 'Arabic' room, with raised cushions and a carpet. Nowadays, ornate furniture is fashionable in Makkah, but most houses still have at least one Arabic room like this one.

Left: Ali Shafy (right) with his cousin Abu Bakr, who has come to visit. Ali is a keen football fan, and proud of his Maradona shirt. Boys in Makkah use any space they can find to play football.

Right: Maryam and baby Raja on the stairs of the Shafy family's new house. You can see a mechanical digger through the staircase window – a sign that the house is not yet finished.

dishes and salads. The meal is followed by fruit and occasionally a sweet, like the milky pudding called *mahalabiyya* flavoured with rosewater, or syrupy pastries called *tarompa.* Then it is time for the afternoon nap.

In the late afternoon Nashwa and Ali do their homework. If there is time, the children watch television or the video, or play around the house until supper and bedtime. On weekday evenings Ramzy goes into town on errands, or to visit friends. He often takes Aisha out to the clothing and gold markets, or to visit her friends or family.

Weekends
In Saudi Arabia, the weekend falls on Thursday and Friday, because Friday is the Muslim day for congregational prayers at the mosque. The Shafy family often go for an outing at the weekend, and they will probably also pay a visit to Ramzy and Aisha's parents. Often there is a wedding or other family celebration for Aisha to attend on Thursday night. These take place very late at night and so she may not return home until dawn.

Building a house
The Shafys have always lived in rented apartments but some years ago they received a loan from the government to build their own home. The loan doesn't cover all the cost of construction, and building is expensive in Saudi Arabia, so the Shafys have been building their house in stops and starts. They stop when they run out of money and start again when they have saved enough to pay the builders some more.

Above: Ramzy Shafy with baby Raja. Raja has the name of *Allah* (God) written on his forehead. This is a custom in Makkah and is done to protect the young child from any unseen evil.

Right: Nashwa and her cousin Sulafa practise Arabic dancing. It is for girls only and they will stop if a man – even their father – comes into the room!

Below: Nashwa puts make-up on Sulafa. The electronic equipment in the background is typical in a Makkan house.

Growing up

Most Makkan children grow up amidst the bustle and commotion of a large family. It is quite common to have as many as five or six brothers and sisters, and of course there are always plenty of other relatives coming and going in any Makkan household. Large families are greatly admired in Makkah, and they are a source of pride.

In a Makkan family, the girls usually share one room and the boys another. However, little children under five or six years old almost always sleep in their parents' room. Even if they have plenty of space, few Makkan parents would think of letting their younger children spend a night alone.

Respect for elders
Makkan children are brought up to obey and respect their parents, and any other older person. Children address an older person as *ammi* (my uncle) or *ammati* (my aunt) as a term of respect, and older people call those younger than themselves *waladi* or *ibni* (my son) or *binti* (my daughter) as a term of endearment.

Right: The pilgrimage is part of growing up in Makkah, and children often perform the pilgrimage rituals with their parents. Pilgrims from other countries also often bring their children with them. This girl, carried above the heads of the crowd, is stoning the pillars at Mina.

Above: Education for girls is a fairly recent thing in Saudi Arabia. Now, however, there are girls' schools in every neighbourhood of Makkah and many young Makkan women go to the local Um Al Qurra university. These girls are wearing a school uniform of green, ankle-length dresses.

Left: During the pilgrimage season, children often help out with the family business. This boy is selling plastic prayer beads.

All Muslims have a special duty to honour their parents – their mothers above anyone else and then their fathers. A famous saying of the Prophet was that, "Paradise lies at the foot of your mother." Children in Makkah are usually very upset if they displease their mother and whether they are still young, or quite grown-up, they rush to make amends.

Growing up with the pilgrimage
The disruptive tumult of the annual pilgrimage is an ordinary part of life for Makkan children. They quickly learn to distinguish all the many nationalities of those who visit their city. They can spot at an instant variations in manner, dress, language and physical appearance. Makkan children know at once whether a hajji comes from Algeria, Tunisia, Turkey, India, Senegal, Kuwait – or anywhere else in the Muslim world.

Below: A Makkan boy on his way to school. On his head he carries books and a prayer carpet. Boys often wear football clothes under their white robes, ready for a quick game at break-time.

Right: There are few playgrounds in Makkah, so boys use any available space to play. These boys are doing a mock sword fight, using sticks, on a stretch of wasteland near their homes.

Going to school

Makkan children start school at the age of six, though younger ones can go to state-run kindergarten. Boys and girls always go to separate schools: co-education does not exist in Saudi Arabia.

Saudi children have to do homework from their very first year at school. Much of it consists of learning *suras,* or chapters, of the Qur'an by heart. In fact, a good deal of the early learning in school revolves around Islamic teachings, though of course there are also lessons in reading, writing and maths. As children approach secondary school, the range of subjects widens out.

Outside school

Makkan schools do not organize activities outside school hours, but there are sports facilities for boys sponsored by the government's Youth Welfare Organization.

Teenagers

In Makkah, as in all Muslim societies, children are considered to be adult when they reach the age of puberty, usually at around 11 or 12 years old. They then formally assume the religious obligations of an adult Muslim. They are required to pray, fast and perform the Hajj. Girls must cover themselves properly, according to Islamic teaching, and boys begin to dress as young men, in the long white robes that are traditional in Saudi Arabia.

There are no discos or similar places where boys and girls can meet. And in any case, young people in their teens are busy preparing for adult life. In addition to their studies, boys become the companions of their fathers, often learning their trade or business. Girls become the companions of their mothers, and begin to take responsibility in running the house.

Above: Girls are discouraged from playing out in public and they are not allowed to mix with boys outside the family. However, the Makkan household is full of activity and there are always plenty of sisters, cousins and neighbourhood friends around to play with. Some Makkan families buy playground equipment for their roof or courtyard, and there is usually a ball or a bicycle around.

Here Nashwa Shafy and her friends play a skipping game on the roof of the Shafy family's new house.

Makkans relaxing

Because it is so terribly hot for most of the year, Makkans rejoice at any kind of coolness. Desert people in general have a great appreciation for the quality of the air, and Makkans are no exception. The most common outdoor recreation in Makkah is simply taking the air.

Taking the air

Every afternoon you can see men of all ages sitting outside their shops or houses, on carpets spread over the ground, or on raised seats called *dhakkahs*. They may be engaged in conversation or some might be reading quietly from the Qur'an. What they are really doing is savouring the last hour of light and enjoying the soft breezes which dampen the furnace of the day.

Women also sit outside to enjoy the air, but within the privacy of their homes. Traditional houses in Makkah have always been built with enclosed yards where women can go outside unveiled, to drink tea and talk.

Some larger houses have a *satooh*, or roof area, which is an especially pleasant, airy place to sit.

Picnics and outings

Family outings are a variation on this practice of taking the air, and picnics are a favourite pastime. At weekends the whole family may go out to an open space to sit and have a meal, or snack of nuts and sweets, and enjoy the air.

The plain of Arafat, where the pilgrims gather during the Hajj, is a favourite place to picnic. There is also the Red Sea coast at Jeddah, where children can play on playground apparatus set out on the waterfront.

Some Makkan families will make the hour's drive up into the mountain city of Taif

Below: From sunset until late at night, *qahwas* (outdoor cafés for men only) are filled with men sitting on high seats (*dhakkahs*), drinking sweet tea or tiny cups of greenish Arabic coffee. There they chat, play cards, watch television – and take the air.

Several of the men in this café are sharing puffs of a sweet-smelling mixture called *jiraak*, which they take from a *shisha*, or large bubbly water-pipe.

Above: The raised cot-like seat, or *dhakkah*, is a common sight in Makkah. Here two men relax on their *dhakkah* and enjoy the afternoon air. The carpet and the hard cushion on which the man on the left reclines are typical – as is the carpet on the pavement below.

Left: Worshippers relax on the roof of the Holy Mosque after *maghrib* (sunset prayer). The roof of the Mosque has only recently been opened. The crane shows that building work continues.

Above: Almost half the television programmes in Makkah are for children. There are cartoons every morning and a favourite children's programme is the Arabic version of *Sesame Street.*

Above: A late-afternoon scene outside a clothes shop in Makkah. You often see a group of men like this sitting outside a shop, relaxing, chatting and enjoying the cooler air late in the day. The man seated in the centre of this group is drinking a glass of tea.

to sit in the gardens there and enjoy the cool mountain air. This is a particularly popular picnic place during the summer months when Taif is cooler than the blazing hot inland cities. There is also a small children's zoo at Taif.

But it is the air that is most important and it is common to see families sitting out in the most unlikely places – on pavements, on the hard shoulder of a motorway, on a barren empty stretch of land – anywhere out in the open where the air can be enjoyed.

Fun for children

There are two amusement parks in Makkah, open every day of the week except at exam times. Zahir Gardens and Misfalah Gardens

have carnival rides and ferris wheels, and are a real treat for children. Parents also take their children – especially girls who are not allowed to play outside alone – to the little garden areas that can be found in the newest suburbs of the city.

Other entertainment

Makkah is different from many other cities in that there is very little public entertainment available. There are no cinemas or art galleries; no nightclubs; no large sports arenas, health clubs or public swimming pools. This is partly because activities of this kind do not belong to Arab tradition, but it is also true that they would not be considered suitable in the holiest city of Islam.

At home

Inside the house, video and television are the most popular forms of entertainment. Video shops in Makkah sell Egyptian, Indian and American films that have been censored by government authorities to make sure they contain no unnecessary violence or immorality.

There are two television channels in Saudi Arabia, one Arabic language and the other mainly English, although there are some French and Hindi programmes as well. Television has become an increasingly important pastime for people because the intensely hot weather drives them into the air-conditioned indoors.

Seasons of the year

Below: Crowds of worshippers around the Ka'bah await the sunset prayer during Ramadan. The orange containers are filled with Zamzam water for people to drink as soon as the sun goes down.

Makkans generally like to spend more time at the Holy Mosque during Ramadan, either attending prayers or just reading the Qu'ran, as the man and boy in the foreground are doing. Makkans also like to perform the *Umrah*, or little pilgrimage during Ramadan – and the most religious men sometimes spend the whole of the last ten days of the month in the Holy Mosque, in a kind of retreat called *i'tikaf*.

In Makkah, as in the rest of Saudi Arabia, the official calendar is the Muslim *Hijriyya* calendar, which is different from the solar (sun) calendar used in the western world.

The months of the *Hijriyya* calendar are timed by the movements of the moon rather than by the movements of the sun. A lunar (moon) year has 354 days, while the solar year has 365 days. This difference means that the twelve months of the *Hijriyya* calendar do not match the twelve months of the solar calendar – and so the Muslim months do not fall in the same season every year. For example, in Britain, January is always winter. But the Muslim month of Ramadan moves through the seasons.

The *Hijriyya* calendar starts counting from the *Hijrah*, when the Prophet Muhammad emigrated from Makkah to Madinah, so Muslims are now in the 15th century After *Hijrah* (AH).

The ninth month of the *Hijriyya* calendar is Ramadan. After Dhul Hijjah (the month of the Hajj) Ramadan is the most popular time to visit Makkah, and towards the end of Ramadan the crowds resemble Hajj-time.

Ramadan

Ramadan is a month of fasting. This means adult Muslims cannot eat or drink during daylight hours. If the month of Ramadan falls during the summer, when the days are long and hot, this can be very hard. But even so, Muslims regard this month as the sweetest most delightful time of the year. In Makkah, where everyone observes the fast, the whole pattern of life changes during Ramadan.

The month begins with cannons booming out over the town from the surrounding mountains and cannons also mark the beginning and end of each day's fast.

During the hour before dawn each day, Makkans eat a meal called *sahur* and then, after the dawn prayer, most people sleep until it is time for work. Working hours are shorter during Ramadan and shops and offices open later than usual. In the afternoon, most people sleep again because they get little sleep during Ramadan nights.

From sunset to dawn, life in Makkah is a swirl of activity. After the sunset prayer, families break their fast with a large meal of traditional Makkan food, and there is often

only just time to finish eating before the night prayer is called. After this, shops open and people go back to work. Most shops stay open until about one hour before dawn.

Those who wish to may stay in the mosque after the night prayer for a special Ramadan prayer called *tarawih*. Then, after *tarawih*, families go out visiting, or shopping, or they entertain guests at home. Ramadan is a festive season and gifts are exchanged, often consisting of food, which is prepared with special care at this time.

Because of all the gift-giving during Ramadan, and because there is an influx of pilgrims, Makkan businesses thrive. Traditionally Makkans have new clothes made for the Eid festival at the end of the month, so tailors and dressmakers are busy.

For the last ten days of Ramadan government offices close so that Makkans can concentrate on their worship. The climax of Ramadan is the 'Night of Power' which falls on one of the last ten nights of the month.

Eid festivals

Makkans celebrate two festivals each year, both called *Eid* festivals. One falls at the end of Ramadan and the other at the end of the

Above: If it rains in Makkah, it rains hard. Streets are quickly flooded – and so are houses if you leave the shutters open! Rain never lasts long though, and this flood will soon drain away.

Hajj. At *Eid*, there are special congregational prayers at the mosque, followed by feasting, thanksgiving, and the exchange of gifts. Children are given *Eid* presents of money or toys. In Makkah, however, *Eid* festivals are relatively subdued. After the tumult of the Hajj and Ramadan, Makkans are happy to take things quietly.

Cool season

The winter in Makkah lasts from about November to February of the solar calendar. Even then it can be hot, but usually the days are warm and the nights cool – occasionally even cold enough to wear a jumper. Muslims planning their pilgrimage sometimes wait until the Hajj month falls during the winter, if only to avoid the dangers of heat-stroke.

The longing for cool is so strong in Makkans that a grey, overcast day brings exclamations of delight. "Halwa" ('how sweet') they say, "what a wonderful day!"

Rains

Rain is rare in Makkah but when it does come it is often with terrifying force. A downpour may last less than ten minutes, but still lead to floods that cause astonishing damage. However, despite its violence, rain is a welcome sight in Makkah, a cause for jubilation in this dry, sun-baked town. People are so happy that families arrange to meet up to enjoy the rainy weather, and there is a special rice and lentil dish made for the occasion 'to keep warm.'

The Boom

The rising price of oil throughout the 1970s brought Saudi Arabia sudden, enormous wealth – so much so that the period is sometimes called the 'Boom'. The money was used instantly to develop the desert nation: roads, schools and hospitals were built, public utilities such as running water, electricity, and telecommunications were improved and extended. Places such as Jeddah and Riyadh were transformed from small traditional Arab towns to sprawling modern cities with skyscrapers, shopping malls, elegant hotels and international restaurants.

Changes in Makkah

In Makkah, the changes have been rather different. Here Saudi Arabia's new-found wealth has been used to tackle problems caused by the rapidly increasing number of pilgrims visiting the city. Between 1955 and 1979 the average number of pilgrims swelled from 200 000 to nearly two million, mainly because commercial air travel made it possible for many more people to make the journey than ever before.

The increase put severe strains on the city of Makkah, which had remained little changed for decades. Cars also became much more widespread during this period, so that at Hajj-time roads became impossibly congested. Water became scarce, and pilgrim accommodation became overcrowded. The only solution was a hugely expensive programme of expansion and renovation of Hajj facilities, which began during the 1970s and still continues.

Whole neighbourhoods were pulled down to make way for these developments. The government paid high prices for the land, so that the people who lived in these areas could move to newly developed suburbs on the outskirts of the town. As a result, the area that Makkah covers has expanded dramatically. Whole sections of barren, stony wasteland have, in the last few years, become brand-new housing developments and shopping districts. New shopping boulevards on the outskirts of town contrast sharply with the narrow winding streets near the Holy Mosque.

Windfall

For many Makkans this sudden development of their city was an enormous windfall. Some families whose grandparents may have acquired a tract of land near to the Holy Mosque simply by marking it out with stones, were paid millions of dollars when the government took it over for its development projects. Many people suddenly found themselves with more money than they had ever hoped for.

Above: Oil-wealth has allowed many young Saudis to indulge in luxuries – like this sports car!

Below: High technology in the centre of Makkah. This bank of telephone booths allows pilgrims to make direct-dial calls anywhere in the world.

This new affluence allowed them to live a life of comfort and ease, quite different from the hardy Makkan lifestyle. They built large modern houses, bought new expensive cars, hired servants from poor Muslim countries and went for holidays abroad.

Even those who didn't strike it rich shared in the prosperity that the Boom brought. Salaries for government employees were raised. Every Saudi was offered a government loan to build a house. And an almost bewildering number of opportunities for opening businesses appeared.

Other effects of the Boom
For Makkah, the Boom brought some problems as well as benefits: many people are now attracted to Makkah because of the employment it offers, rather than just because of their religion, and some people feel this has affected the pious atmosphere of the city; the sudden sophistication that money brought young Makkans has sometimes conflicted with the old ways that they were brought up to respect; and many parts of old Makkah were destroyed when the beautiful old traditional houses were replaced by the drab high-rises and flyovers.

However, Makkah has not become nearly as westernized as other Saudi-Arabian towns, and remains essentially what it always was: Islam's most sacred city. The main effects of the changes are that life is easier and the pilgrimage is a safer, healthier, more organized and generally more pleasant experience than it was in the past.

Above: From the 1950's onwards the number of pilgrims visiting Makkah increased enormously. To begin with, this increase led to terrible traffic congestion around the Holy Mosque and on the roads to and from the sacred area outide the town. To relieve the congestion, an elaborate tunnel and road system was cut through and over the stony, mountainous terrain.

Neighbouring places

There has always been a strong relationship between Makkah and its neighbouring cities, and that relationship has grown stronger as communications and roads have improved.

Madinah

Although they lie nearly 500 kilometres apart, Makkah and its sister city Madinah are closely related because of their religious history and tradition. Madinah contains the tomb of the Prophet Muhammad and his Mosque, the second Holy Mosque of Islam, making this oasis town the second city of Islam. Madinah is almost always visited by pilgrims, before or after their stay in Makkah.

Madinah has always been thought of as a sweeter, more gentle place than the rough and majestic pilgrimage centre of Makkah. This may not be strictly true, but there is a noticeable difference in the character of the two holy places and, for a change of religious pace, many Makkans like to spend their holidays in Madinah.

Jeddah

Much closer to Makkah, about 80 kilometres to the west, lies the port city of Jeddah. The vast majority of all visitors to Makkah, whether they arrive by sea or air, pass through Jeddah first.

Many Makkans commute daily to Jeddah to work, and some families have even settled there, keeping on their family houses in Makkah where they visit their parents and grandparents at weekends. During the Boom, Jeddah became much more modern than Makkah, and Makkans often make the short trip to Jeddah (about 40 minutes on the superhighway) to enjoy its glittering new shopping malls and restaurants. Many families make a point of taking their children to Jeddah, to visit its amusement parks, swimming pools and large playgrounds. For Makkans, visiting Jeddah is like going to the big city.

Taif

Taif is a town in the mountains high above Makkah. In summer it is pleasantly cool and in winter it is very cold, sometimes even snowy. Because of its climate Taif is the Saudi government's summer capital.

Even before the coming of Islam, many wealthy Makkans had gardens and summer residences in Taif and the same is still true today.

Surrounding villages

Just outside the sacred precinct that surrounds Makkah there are still many villages which are the traditional homes of the desert tribes. The tribes, though mostly settled in towns and villages today, still

Below: Madinah is the sister city of Makkah. It is called the 'City of the Prophet' because it was here that Muhammad lived out his life, and here that he died. His tomb lies beneath this green dome, which has come to represent Madinah to the rest of the Muslim world.

retain many of the customs that come from their age-old nomadic tradition. The people of each tribe still stick together, problems are still referred to a council of elders, lamb and rice are still the staple diet. The people are proud of their heritage and of their family lineage (which they can often trace back thousands of years) and they tend to feel superior to city people of mixed background.

Of course, village life has changed with the new age of oil, and most people have long since exchanged their camels for Japanese trucks and their black tents for concrete houses. They watch television, their children go to schools and universities and they engage in business – but still it is not unusual for a village girl to kick her shoes off after school and go out to tend the family's sheep in the afternoons.

Legend

▬▬▬ ▬ ▬ ▬	Main roads and tunnels
▬▬▬ ▬ ▬ ▬	Ring roads and tunnels
▬▬▬ ▬ ▬ ▬	Pedestrian walkways and tunnels
▬▬▬	Built-up area

0   1   2   kilometres

1. Setteen Street – one of the fashionable new shopping streets on the outskirts of town.

2. Mansour Street is the centre of the Nigerian community.

3. Misfalah Gardens has an amusement park for children.

4. The original *halaqa* (fruit and vegetable market) is in the Jarwal district.

5. Shamiyya, the main Indonesian district of Makkah, is on high ground near the Holy Mosque.

6. The buildings of the Holy Mosque surround the Ka'bah. The straight part of the building, on the right, covers the course of the *sa'i* which runs between the hills of Safa and Marwah.

6a. Pilgrims try to touch or kiss the Black Stone, set in one corner of the Ka'bah, because the Prophet did so.

3rd ring road

Zahir

1

4

Jarwal

5

6

Shubaikah

2

2nd ring road   Aj

3

Misfalah

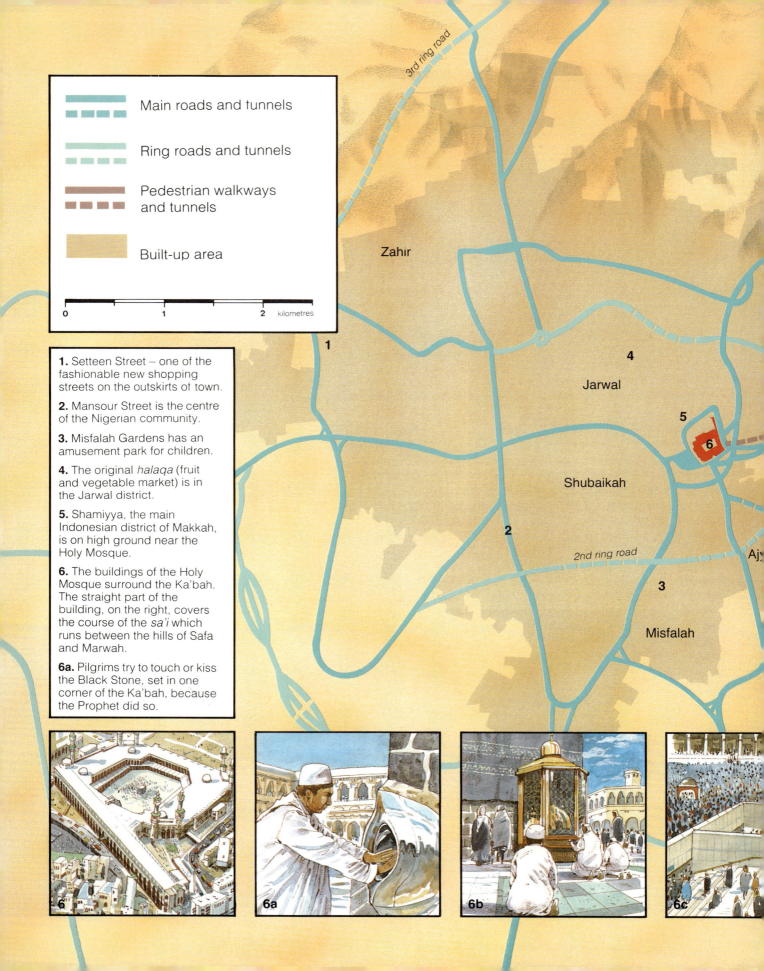

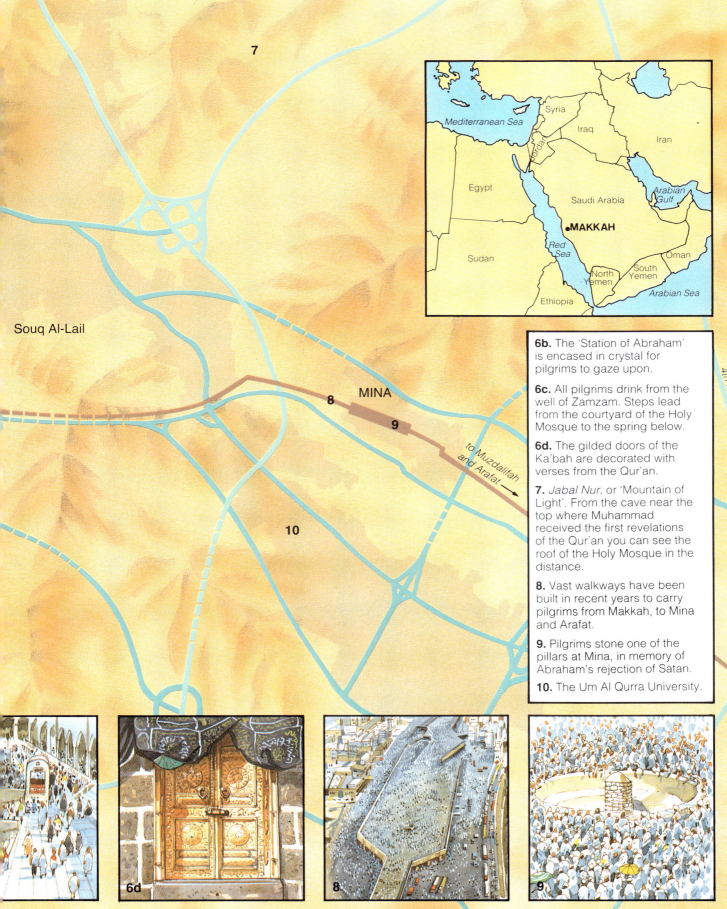

7

Souq Al-Lail

MINA

8

9

10

to Muzdalifah and Arafat →

4th ring road

Map inset (Middle East):

Mediterranean Sea

Syria

Iraq

Iran

Jordan

Egypt

Saudi Arabia

Arabian Gulf

●MAKKAH

Red Sea

Sudan

Oman

North Yemen

South Yemen

Ethiopia

Arabian Sea

6b. The 'Station of Abraham' is encased in crystal for pilgrims to gaze upon.

6c. All pilgrims drink from the well of Zamzam. Steps lead from the courtyard of the Holy Mosque to the spring below.

6d. The gilded doors of the Ka'bah are decorated with verses from the Qur'an.

7. *Jabal Nur*, or 'Mountain of Light'. From the cave near the top where Muhammad received the first revelations of the Qur'an you can see the roof of the Holy Mosque in the distance.

8. Vast walkways have been built in recent years to carry pilgrims from Makkah, to Mina and Arafat.

9. Pilgrims stone one of the pillars at Mina, in memory of Abraham's rejection of Satan.

10. The Um Al Qurra University.

6d

8

9

The Arabic language

Arabic is an ancient language, similar in many ways to other ancient languages such as Hebrew (the language of the ancient Jews.) Today, there are over 60 million people in the world who speak Arabic as their native language. Most of them live in North Africa and the Middle East. But all Muslims, wherever they live, learn Arabic because it is the language of the Qur'an.

At the time of the Prophet Muhammad, Arabic was already a beautiful and highly-refined language. It was spoken rather than written down, and the Arabs were known for their marvellous poetry. However, when the people of Makkah first heard the words of the Qur'an, many of them were immediately convinced that such beautiful language could not have been composed by a poet – or by any human being for that matter. Muslims still believe that the beauty of the language of the Qur'an shows that it comes straight from God.

Arabic (like Hebrew) is written from right to left. It is also a phonetic language, which means that each letter corresponds to an exact sound. There are 28 sounds, or letters, in the Arabic alphabet. 14 are called 'sun' letters and 14 are called 'moon' letters. 'Root' words are usually made up of three letters. From these roots, many interrelated words are formed.

For example, كتاب (kitab) means a piece of writing, record, letter or book. مكتب (maktab) is an office, or study. مكتبة (maktaba) is a bookshop. كاتب (katib) is a clerk, or scribe and so on.

Some Arabic words used in this book

abaya black, flowing cape-like garment worn by Saudi women.

Allah The Arabic word for God. Literally, *the* God.

ammi; ammati my uncle; my aunt. Terms used by children to address an older person.

asr the afternoon prayer.

dhur the noon prayer.

binti; ibni, wala'di my daughter; my son. Terms of endearment used by older people when addressing a child.

dhakkah raised outdoor seat.

farah wedding party.

Hajj the pilgrimage to Makkah.

haram sacred and forbidden. Makkah and the surrounding area are *haram*. The Haram refers to the Holy Mosque itself.

Hijrah the Prophet's departure from Makkah to Madinah. The Muslim *Hijriyya* calendar starts from this point.

ihram two pieces of cloth, usually white, that pilgrims must wear as they perform the Hajj.

isha the night prayer.

kiswat the huge black silk cloth that covers the Ka'bah.

kuftia embroidered prayer-cap worn by Saudi men.

maghrib the sunset prayer.

milka wedding ceremony.

mutawif pilgrim guide. One who leads people on the *tawaf*.

qahwa outdoor cafe (for men only).

sa'i running between the hills of Safa and Marwah as part of the *Umrah* or the Hajj.

satooh roof area, or garden.

sahur the meal eaten before dawn during Ramadan.

shumach red and white checked cloth that Saudi men wear on their heads. A similar white cloth is called a *ghutra*. Both are held in place by a black circular *egaal*.

sharshif voluminous white scarf that women wear for prayer at home, or if a male guest visits the house.

shisha bubbly water pipe, from which a group of men may share puffs of a sweet-smelling mixture called *jiraak*.

souq traditional Arab market.

subh the dawn prayer.

tawaf circling the Ka'bah seven times as part of the Hajj or *Umrah*.

thobe long white robe worn by Saudi men.

Umrah smaller pilgrimage, that Muslims may undertake at any time of the year.

Books to read

There are very few other books about Makkah and none specially written for young readers. However, there are a number of books about Islam, including *The Muslim World* by Richard Tames (Macdonald, 1982). Also, *The Life of the Prophet Muhammad* by Leila Azzam and Aisha Gouverneur (Islamic Texts Society, 1985) is a readable and authoratative account of the life of the Prophet.

For a broader look at Saudi Arabia and other Middle-Eastern countries there is *The Middle East* by Maureen Smallwood Abdallah (Macdonald Countries Series – revised edition, 1987).

Index

Numbers in heavy type refer to picture captions, or to the pictures themselves.

abaya 29, 44
Abdul Aziz Ibn Saud 15, **15**
Abraha, general 16
Abraham 10, 17, 18, **43**
Africans 21
Ajyad 22, **42**
Al-Hajj **6**, 8, 12, 18, **18**, 19, **19**, 24, **24**, 33, 34, 36, 37, 38, 44
Arabian Peninsula **14**, 15
Arabic **12**, **13**, 16, **17**, 20, 21, **30**, 35, **35**, 44
Arabic calligraphy **4**, 6, **12**, **17**
Arabic dancing **31**
Arafat, plain of 16, 18, **18**, 19, **19**, 34, **43**
asr 26, 44

Battle of the Elephant 16
Baghdad 14
bedouin **10**, 11
Black Stone 16
Boom 15, 38, 39, 40, **42**

cafés (*qahwas*) **34**
camels **10**, 11, 41
caravans 11, 12, 15
Central Asians 21

Damascus 14
dhakkah 34, **34**
Dhul Hijjah 18, 36
dhuhr 26, 44
dress 7, 25, 28, 29, 33, **33**
desert 8, **8**, **10**, 11, 14

Eid festivals 37
Ethiopia 13
food 22, **22**, 23, 24, **26**, **28**, **29**, 30, 31, 36, 37, 41

ghutra 28, 44
gold **22**

Hagar 10, 18
Hajj *see* Al-Hajj
Hijrah 13, 36
Hijriyya calendar 36
Holy Mosque **6**, **8**, **9**, 15, **15**, 16, 17, **17**, 18, 19, 21, 22, **23**, 26, 30, **36**, 37, 38, **39**, **42–43**
homes 11, 15, 21, 27, 28, **28**, 29, **29**, 30, **30**, 31, **31**, 33, **33**, 34, **34**, 39, 40

Ibn Saud 15, **15**
idol worship 11, **11**, 12, 13
ihram 18, **19**, 44
Indians 21
Indonesians 21, **21**, **25**, 30
isha 26, 44
Ishmael 10
Islam 8, **11**, 12, 13, 14, **15**, 20, 22, 28, 33, 35, 39, 40
Istanbul 14

Jabal Nur **12**, **43**
Jahiliyya 10
Jawa 21
Jeddah 34, 38, 40, 41
jiraak **34**, 44

Ka'bah **6**, 8, **9**, **10**, 11, **11**, 13, **14**, 15, **15**, 16, **16**, 17, **17**, 18, 20, 24, **27**, **36**, **42**, 44
Khadija 12
Khalifs 14
Kiswat 16, **16**, **17**, 44
kuftias **25**, 44

Madinah 9, 13, 14, 15, 36, 40, **40**
maghrib 26, **27**, 35, 44
Makkah time 26
Mansour Street **20**, **42**
markets 21, 22, **22**, **26**, 31, **41**
marriage 28
Marwah 10, **16**, 18, **18**, **42**
Mina, valley of 19, **19**, **32**, **43**
Misfalah 22, **42**
money-changers **24**
Mosque *see* Holy Mosque
Mount of Mercy **18**
Mughal Empire 14
Muhammad *see* Prophet Muhammad
Muhammad Ibn Saud 15
Muslims 8, 9, **9**, 12, 13, **13**, 14, **14**, 15, 16, **17**, 20, 22, **25**, 28, 32, 36, **40**, 44
mutawif (pilgrim guide) 24, 25, 30
Muzdalifah 18

Nigerians 20, 21, **21**
Night of Power 37
nomadic tribes 10, 11, 12, 15, 41

oil 15, 24, 38, **38**, 41
Ottoman Empire 14

parks & gardens 35, 40
perfumeries **23**
Persian **10**, 14
Persian Empire 14
picnics **29**, 34, 35
pilgrimage **8**, 15, **16**, **17**, 18, 19, **19**, **21**, **23**, 24, **24**, 25, **25**, **32**, 37, 38, **38**, 39, 40
pilgrims **6**, 8, 10, 11, 15, **16**, 18, 19, 20, 22, 23, 24, **24**, 25, **32**, 39, 40, **42**, 44
pillars of faith' 12
prayer 8, 16, 17, 18, **18**, 26, **26**, 29, 30, 33, **33**, 36, 37, 44
Prophet Muhammad 8, 10, 11, **11**, 12, **12**, 13, **13**, 14, **15**, 16, 18, **23**, 32, 36, 40, **40**, **42–43**, 44

Qur'an **5**, **6**, 12, **12**, **13**, 16, 17, **17**, **19**, 24, **25**, **26**, 33, 34, **36**, **43**, 44

Ramadan 12, 36, **36**, 44
Red Sea 34, **41**
Riyadh 38
roads/streets 8, **9**, 20, **27**, 35, **37**, **39**, 41, **42–43**

Safa 10, **16**, 18, **18**, **42**
sa'i 18, **18**
servants 30, 39
school 8, 30, **32**, 33. **33**, 38, 41
sharshif 29, 44
shisha **34**, 44
shopping 22, **22**, 23, **23**, **26**, **27**, **28**, 31, 37, 38, 40, 41
shops **5**, **6**, **7**, 22, 23, 26, 27, 28, 35, **35**
Shubaikah 22, **42**
shumach 28, 44
Souq Al Lail (night market) 22, 44
souvenirs 24, **25**
sport 30, 33, **33**
Station of Abraham 16, **42–43**
subh 26, 44

Taif 34, 35, 40
Takarna 21
tawaf 18, **18**, 24
television 35, 40
tents 11, 18, **19**
thobe 28, 44

Umrah **16**, **17**, **36**, 44

veils **23**, 29

wedding ceremony (*milka*) 28, 44
wedding party (*farah*) 28, 31, 44

Yathrib 13
Yemen 10, **10**, 11, 21, **23**

Zamzan, well of 10, **27**, **36**, **42–43**

PRINTED IN BELGIUM BY
proost
INTERNATIONAL BOOK PRODUCTION